July 2007

Best Wishes

[signature]

The Minimax Gui

GW00367974

The Tarot & You

BMC
PUBLISHING

Minimax Guide To The Tarot & You

Published by:
BMC Publishing
PO Box 932
Naas
Co. Kildare
Republic of Ireland

For sales enquiries and re seller information including bulk discounts please contact:
sales@bmcpublish.com

ISBN: 978-1-906135-01-0

Printed in the United Kingdom

Page layout & cover design: D 4 Design

www.bmcpublish.com

The Tarot
& You

By
Brett Campbell

Introduction

One question I hear frequently as a tarot card reader is 'Do you have to have a gift to be able to read cards?' My answer to this is always the same, anyone who is prepared to study the cards with an open mind, relate to the pictures and put meaning into the pictures will be able to read them successfully. When a reader is blessed with the gift of clairvoyance, card readings can become a lot more insightful for the person having the reading, but no gift is actually necessary for one to read tarot cards well.

Learning to read and interpret tarot cards can be a meaningful and rewarding task. It can also be a confusing and tiresome drag if you don't know how to do it. There are hundreds, if not thousands of books on the tarot, covering everything from basic and sometimes not so basic meanings of the cards, to spells that can be used to enhance or change your everyday life. One subject that one seldom comes across is how to find your own 'voice' in card interpretations, instead of learning other people's interpretations and using these to do readings. You will read in books that you are supposed to meditate on the cards, but I know from my own experience that the word 'meditate' put me off even trying. It took me years of working with the cards to find out how they wished to be interpreted, and the basic steps I describe in this book are written taking this into account, and of course, leaving out all the exercises that did not work or help.

I might add here that the meanings that I have for the cards which you will find in the last chapter of this book were derived by myself after reading numerous books on the subject, studying the cards in great detail and then using the method that I describe in this book to come to the finished product. These meanings are by no means law, and I strongly urge each and every person who reads this book to perform the exercises described in order to find their own 'voice'.

Chapter 1

About this book

This book is not your average tarot book with card meanings to learn off by heart and follow without question. It is a book that leads you down a path of enlightenment, prompting you to find out how certain cards will affect you and make you feel, exploring the emotions that will be stirred within you by examining the pictures on the cards and therefore making your own decisions on what cards mean and how you should interpret them. The meaning I have included in the last chapter should be used only as a guide to get you going along the right track. You will often find that after a couple of weeks of studying the cards, the same card will have evoked the same feeling or response in you over and over again. This is what I mean by finding your own voice. Take time out of every day to study the cards, see what responses they evoke in you and write them down. More often than not, you will find patterns in your feelings towards certain cards. Very seldom are these feelings or responses far from the studied meaning of the card itself. So if you are looking for a rewarding adventure of the soul, continue reading this guide as it can take you on a journey that will enrich your life and help many people along the way. Just always remember one thing – a properly interpreted spread can bring hope and guidance to an inquirer, whereas a poorly read spread can be disastrous, as can a spread that is interpreted with a hidden agenda. Do not abuse these cards, and don't read for an inquirer until you are quite confident that you fully understand the meaning of each card.

Chapter 2

About The Tarot

The tarot deck consists of 78 cards, 56 of these are called the minor arcana, the remaining 22 the major arcana or trump cards. The minor arcana is divided into suits called Wands, Cups, Swords and Pentacles, each suit having one through ten and then a Knight, Page, King and Queen which are referred to as the court cards.

The major arcana has twenty two cards, starting with The Fool at number 0 or 1 and ending with The Universe at 21 or 22. The names and order of these trumps may vary from deck to deck, and the pictures portraying the major arcana are often more detailed than those portraying the minor arcana.

No one is quite sure when or how tarot card came to be, the earliest known source being a deck from 15 century Italy. Adding to its mystique, no one is quite sure whether it originated as a game or a method of divination. Over the years it has been outlawed by certain people and religious groups as evil, but in recent years has come to be more socially acceptable and has become quite popular with people seeking guidance in everyday life matters. However, after saying this, I think I should make it quite clear that it is not a fool proof method to live your life by. It can be useful as a guidance tool, but should never be followed word for word. Take what you need out of a reading and remember, a lot that does not seem relevant at the time could prove to be relevant in time to come, but never allow cards and their meanings to rule your life!

Chapter 3

Spreads and how to read them

Over the years, many different spreads have been derived and used by readers to interpret cards. Each reader will have their own personal favourite, it is up to the reader to choose which one they feel most comfortable using. When laying out cards, some will often be reversed or upside down, signifying that the meaning could be changed, perhaps even the opposite of the cards normal meaning. It is up to the reader to understand the flow of the reading and make the necessary adjustments to the meaning of the reversed card. In my experience, reversed cards seldom change anything, and I have therefore not included any meaning of reversed cards in the 'card meanings' section of this book.

The spreads we are going to focus on are:
1. The Celtic or Grand cross (probably the most commonly used spread)
2. The Seven Card layout
3. The Decision spread
4. The Master Spread

The Celtic cross

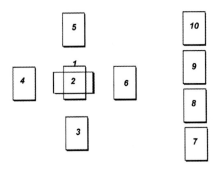

Positions:

1. (Beneath the 2 card, as displayed in the diagram above) Current situation. It represents the general tone of the reading and identifies the problem for the inquirer.
2. Crosses the current situation, showing challenges or obstacles that are facing the inquirer.
3. Subconscious. How the inquirer feels about the matter.
4. First of the past. Recent events that would have influenced or effected the matter.
5. Conscious. The inquirer's feelings about the situation

6. First of the future. Something of significance that will happen in the near future.
7. The Inquirer. The inquirer's role in the situation.
8. The present environment. How people and places are effecting the inquirer with regards the situation
9. Hopes and fears. The inquirers views on the possible outcome of the situation
10. Final outcome. What will happen in order to resolve the situation.

The Celtic cross is used to detect and work on specific problems or situations. It is generally used to guide an inquirer who is experiencing a problem and doesn't know which way to go with it.

7 card layout

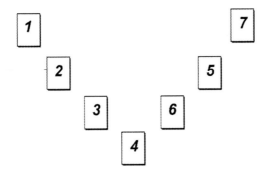

If you are looking for a quick answer to specific problem, this spread could be used

- Shuffle the cards and fan them out in front you, face down.
- The inquirer draws seven cards towards them with their left (heart) hand. Do not turn them face up.
- The reader shuffles these seven cards and lays them out as shown in the diagram above.
- The reader will turn them over, one by one, as the first one is read, the second will be turned up and so on.

Interpretation
      1. Shows the past, or the end of something
      2. Shows the present situation
      3. Shows the future, or the start of something
      4. Shows where you should go from here
      5. Things that will help on hinder you on your quest/journey
      6. Represents what you hope to achieve, and what you fear along the way
      7. The outcome

Decisions spread

A quick way to get direction where there is an important decision to be made and the inquirer is not sure what to do.

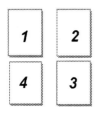

Card 1 – What you should do in advance to achieve your goal.
Card 2 – Things that will get in the way of your progress.
Card 3 – Influences along the way that will mislead or confuse you.
Card 4 – Whatever card comes up here will signify something that you did not expect, an added bonus.

The Master spread

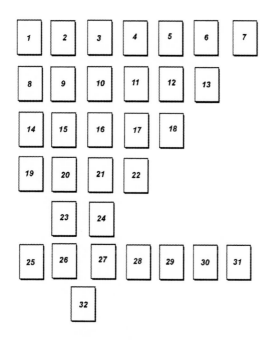

32 cards laid out from left to right as above, turned over and read in numerical order.

Cards 1-7 Previous events that have had a influence on the present situation
Cards 8-13 Present situation
Cards 14-18 Shows involvement of outside

influences (people)
Cards 19-22 The outcome of the situation at best
Cards 23-24   Things that you will learn to your surprise about the matter in question
Cards 25-31 What will happen in the future before the final outcome
Card 32 The outcome.

As I said earlier, everyone has their own method of reading, and their own favourite way of laying out cards. The more you work with the cards, the better your understanding of them will become. I sometimes read three cards at a time, laid out next to each other. When I have finished with the first three, I lay out another three below the first three and read these. I will keep doing this until things stop making sense, or I can no longer see anything meaningful in the cards. I then stop and ask the inquirer to shuffle the cards again, after which I repeat the same layout again and again until I am satisfied that I have exhausted all avenues. This is a method of reading that works quite well for me, although I know readers who have tried it and not had the same positive results that I have.

Chapter 4

Methods of learning to interpret cards

Learning the meanings and interpretations of a deck of Tarot cards if you don't have a sure fire plan of action can be a time consuming, mind-numbing experience that leaves even the most resilient person feeling drained and despondent. The method described in this book is a method I have used, and have passed on to numerous people who have found it to be an effective and enjoyable way of remembering what the cards mean and how to interpret them. Before you start, here are a couple of points that you should remember:

1.   Don't do too much at one sitting.
2.   Never cross your legs while working with cards.
3.   As I said in an earlier chapter, as the different suits relate to different things, when you begin you should study the cards one suit at a time to try and maintain a rhythm in a certain subject.
4.   Only study the cards when you know you will have an uninterrupted period of quite. Don't try to snatch a few moments in between the kids doing their homework and cooking the dinner.

5.   Always have the relevant card that you are reading about in front of you so that you can study the picture while you are reading about it. This is very important, it not only gets you to see the small detail of the cards picture, but as you start reading for people you will find it easier to remember the meanings of the card if you have can relate different aspects of text to different parts of the picture. For example, the fool is stepping off a cliff, but there is a little dog barking up at him as if to warn him of some danger, but he does it anyway as this is his character.

6.   Never be negative about a card. A good example of this is the death card. Drawing the death card in a reading does not necessarily portray a person's death. It can be the death of negativity in a person, death of an old unwanted habit like smoking, death of an old way of life etc. Try and bring a positive edge into all the cards at all times. Remember, these cards are given to us to help, not to instil depression and gloom into the person you are reading for.

7.   As you become more confident with reading, abstract thoughts will enter your mind while you are reading. Even if they have no relevance on what you are saying at that time, get them out there, if you wait you are likely to forget and these 'ideas' give the inquirer that little bit extra.

Method:

First Exercise
Shuffle the cards well. Take each card one at a time, look over them briefly and write down the first three words that come to mind as you look at them. Then find the interpretation of the card in the last chapter of this book and read it carefully. Do not try and find your words in the cards interpretation, but constantly refer to the picture on the card while you are reading the interpretation. You will nearly always be able to find a reason in the interpretation why you thought of that word while you were holding the card. This is the first and most important step to understanding the cards and what they inspire in you.

Second exercise
Take each card, study for thirty seconds, then write the emotions that the card inspired in you at that time. Again, find the interpretation of the card in the last chapter of this book and read it, comparing what your emotion to the meaning of the card. This exercise should be done on a regular basis, and even although I have been reading cards for years, I still do it at least a couple of times a year.

Third exercise
Take each card and study it intensely. What do you see in the card? Describe the picture down to the smallest detail. Then read the meaning and try and

put what you have seen and the meaning of the card together into a story that fits into the picture. This will help you to put meanings to the pictures of the cards when you are doing a reading.

Remember – the more you work with the cards, the more knowledge and understanding you will gain from them.

Chapter 5

Meanings of the cards

The reader should use these notes as a basis of the meanings of the cards. Remember, the idea here is not to learn off by heart the meanings of the cards, but to follow your own instinct and emotion when you are working with them. This way, you will develop your own 'voice' when it comes to reading the cards. Each card has a meaning, but every individual will find their own way to express this meaning in each and every card. If these exercises are taken seriously and instructions are followed to every detail, most of the time you will be surprised how accurate your thoughts on these cards actually are.

Before we begin, there are two cards in this deck that seem to evoke fear and panic in most people, so lets get them out of the way right now. These are The death card and The Devil. These two cards should never be taken for what they are called, but should open doors to a large amount of possibilities. The presents of the Death card , for instance will not mean that someone will die, but rather signifies opportunity for change, and lets face it, change is what life is all about.. Often death may appear after a period of difficulty, or a loss of a friend or lover. The Devil will appear when the inquirer will not face up to something that he or she has to face up to in order to move forward. The devil can also signify temptation or an over indulgence in sensual pleasure.

This section of the book is double spaced, as you may want to add your own notes on each card for future reference.

The Major Arcana

The Fool

Key words – oblivious, happy, seeking something, not always using common sense.

As the first card in the major arcana, the fool portrays the innocents and enthusiasm one begins a journey with. The fool is neither positive nor negative, he just plunges into the unknown without a care in the world, not caring what others say as he does what he feels right for him without considering the outcome. He is sometimes childlike in his innocents and ability to forgive. He has total faith in himself and his actions, never analysing his experiences or allowing them to dictate his next move. The fool will make the same mistake over and over again without caring. The fool almost always stands for new beginnings, new experiences and choices. You yourself have the power to control your destiny. Never allow anyone to control it for you. The fool portrays you living in the present and trusting yourself.

The Magician

Key words – power, manipulation, cunning.

Just as the fool lacks the ambition to be powerful, the Magician has the ability to take power from everything and use it to his advantage. Do not be fooled by the name, there is nothing magical about this card. It simply portrays a powerful person who will stop at nothing to get what they want. This person will never let you know their true intentions. They appear in the most unlikely places and no one ever knows quite what they are up to. The thing you should be aware of is that the Magician works for himself, making sure that he manipulates the world to his own advantage. Ultimately, what this card is trying to say is that you make your own chances in life, so go ahead and do so, because no one else can or will do this for you.

The High Priestess

Key words - decisions, inner feelings, trust.

This is a difficult card to understand. The best way to describe The High Priestess is to say that she represents the potential that is locked into every living being. She also represents the balance that keeps apart positive and negative. Unlike the Magician who uses power outwardly to make changes in the world, the high priestess portrays the potential for power within a person, power that can be used to transform oneself. This card will nearly always appear in a reading where someone needs to make a decision. The card informs the reader that the decision is on the way, but the reader will have to identify the decision and react on it themselves. This is where the inner argument starts, should I - or should I not. Examine the facts and trust your instinct. Listen to the whispers of your own subconscious and make sure you fully understand all the implications before you make your decision.

The Empress

Key words – creative, loving, mother figure, new

beginnings, mature.

The empress represents all that is pure and beautiful about the earth. If Mother Nature was a person, it would be the Empress. Often when the Empress appears in a reading, she is trying to tell us to slow down, take time out to enjoy the aspects of the great outdoors, to use an old cliche, 'smell the roses'. She symbolizes unconditional love, something that can give comfort, but can also become stifling if experienced for great periods of time. This card is often associated with conception and birth. The Empress can show a man, that he has found his soul mate. For a woman, this card can mean that she has finally found or is finding her self-worth.

The Emperor
Key words – law & order, power, ruthlessness, father figure.

The appearance of the Emperor in a reading will often indicate an encounter with the law, being police, government officials, lawyers, etc. Unlike the Empress, he thinks with his mind and not with his heart. He will analyse a situation before acting upon it. He rules with a firm, fair hand. He will always abide by the rules, and his presents in a spread shows us that every rule has a reason. This card signifies freedom to mature and recognize those with needs around you. It can also symbolize someone in a high position with extreme organizational skills.

The Hierophant

Key words – Secret knowledge, Holy man, leader, teacher, mentor.

A stickler for tradition, the Hierophant can be described as one who has a deep respect for his beliefs, but will not blindly follow them to his own ruin. This card portrays a person who will teach you something, possibly but not necessarily about religion, or about your occupation or relationship. It represents the highest possible love in relationship issues, requiring you to open your heart devoid of ego.

The Lovers

Key words – love, togetherness, decisions.

Not always a happy card as it would seem when it appears in a reading. Remember that love can be a wonderful thing, but it can also tear people apart. When this card is found at the beginning of a reading, it can often be sour by the end, and visa versa. It can also portray decision to be made that may or may not have anything to do with matters of the heart. A choice between two paths is another direction this card can take in a reading. This card should be handled with care, and consideration for the cards around it should be taken into account when it is found in a reading.

The Chariot

Key words – discipline, balance, achievement, success, belief in oneself.

The Chariot symbolizes the progression of the inquirers life. It is being pulled along by one white sphinx and one black. One portrays good emotion, the other bad. Without the sphinxes, the chariot could not move forward. Without these emotions, we could not move forward. Un-harnessed, they would run amok. It is up to you to bring them both under control. Learn to harness these emotions and you will be well on your way to achieving great things. When this card appears in love matters, it brings a simple message. Your life is on the road to the place it should be going. Go with and enjoy the ride, as there is very little one can do to speed it along.

Strength

Key words – self control, courage, optimism, energy, willpower.

This card implies that now is the right time to change your situation for the better, whether it be giving up smoking, pulling through a tough emotional time or illness, or making a job decision that you have been putting off, now is the time to do it. You have the inner strength and courage at the moment to be able to see things through without a problem so gather your strength and get on with it. Rid yourself of all crutches and other things you have learned to rely on. This card sometimes signifies the presents of another person who will give you the strength to do what you have to do. However, be disciplined and listen to your inner voice. Avoid temptation, although at this time you will be able to overcome it.

The Hermit

Key words: privacy, being alone, secretive, withdrawn.

This card normally appears when a person needs some time and space to themselves. It can be that the person needs to withdraw into themselves for a period of soul searching or looking into ones self for answers that need to be clarified. The Hermit can also represent a period of stubbornness, a refusal for help or advise when it would be beneficial. Don't be too hasty. Think long and hard before making any decisions.

The Wheel of Fortune
Key words: Destiny, a special gain, luck, end of a problem, an unexpected events, advancement, progress, fortune.

The presents of the wheel implies that good fortune is coming your way. You won't even need to go out and find it; it will find you. It will present itself in front of you, there for the taking, all you have to do is reach out and take it. Like the chariot, this card signifies that things are on the way up and going your way. Just always remember, it is just as easy to loose things if they have come to you easily. While the wheel always appears in a reading as being 'on the way up', at some time it will have to go down, make sure you are ready for this. If this card presents itself to someone looking for an answer, the person should take a step away from their situation and take a good look from an outsider's point of view, as the answer is there for the taking, as clear as daylight to anyone who cares to look.

Justice

Key words: Balance, justice.

Justice is the double edged sword that can cut from both sides. If this card appears in a spread where there is a legal matter, it is saying that it would be wise to make sure that you have all bases covered, that you have looked at the issues from all angles, that you have exhausted all angles, because little things have a way of popping up and ruining even the best laid plans. Justice has no preference; it examines the evidence and makes a decision on pure fact. Make sure you have your facts straight, with no room for human feeling or emotion.

The Hanged Man

Key words: limbo, sacrifice.

You are stuck in a rut because you are ridged and refuse to bend. You are at a point in your life where you have to sacrifice something in order to move forward. If you do not, you will remain in this state of limbo. As you begin to change things, you realise that it is for the better and this will encourage you to change more. In love matters, you will have to compromise your ego in order to make a union work, or drop a relationship that is not living up to your ideals. Remember that although you feel at the beginning that the sacrifice is too much, you will be happier in the long run. Without sacrifice, you cannot move forward, without moving forward, you are stuck in limbo, a place no one wants to be.

Death

Key words: End of something significant.

This is probably one of the most feared cards in the deck, but it should not be. The meaning of this card is not always physical death; it is normally the end of something that has significantly altered your life, like a relationship or job, or even a bad habit. It is better to view this card as a new opportunity, the opening of a door, rather than loss and the closing of one.

Temperance

Key words: good health, harmony, confidence, balance.

Often called the guardian angel, this card brings with it a certain amount of piece and harmony. Enjoy life to the fullest, remembering that everything has to be balanced to maintain the harmony that you will experience. This could mean that you will have to find middle ground rather than argue your opinions too strongly. You would be wise to adjust your thoughts to suit present circumstances to keep a healthy balance.

The Devil

Key words: greed, lust, hedonism, addiction.

A relatively feared card, as the Devil normally represents to worst kind of evil. In fact, all the Devil in this deck represents is temptation that will be put in your way, or overindulgence in sensual pleasures. The bottom line of this card is wanting more, although it can also represent a person who is too conservative, a kind of message to get them to open up a bit more – be a little more adventurous or compulsive. Another way of looking at this card is that the inquirer could be blocked in some way, and will have to learn to let go of something before they can become unblocked and move forward in their lives.

The Tower

Key words: loss, disruption, conflict, shattered dreams, huge change, destruction.

In most cases, this card will portray the end of a friendship or love affair. In money matters, it appears when things are going to get worse; bankruptcy and loss of security are typical issues that this card deal with. A sudden move of job or house are also normally associated with the Tower. The message here is to pick up the pieces and get on with it, as your circumstances can only get better.

The Star

Key words: Faith, optimism, hope.

Just as the Tower deals with destruction of everyday existence, the Star brings hope and renewal to those going through tough times. Old wounds will start to heal, leaving you feeling refreshed and fulfilled. A new cycle is beginning, and you have taken the right path at the crossroads. Symbolizing restoration of order and piece. If you have been hoping for something special to happen, this would be the card to pull.

The Moon

Key words: danger, trickery, illusion, error, deception.

Often found in a reading where the person requesting the reading is involved in fiction writing or acting. The moon is an unknown quantity, bringing with it confusion that cannot be rushed into sense. It will all become clear in the not too distant future, trying to rush answers to clear the confusion will only result in the inquirer becoming more confused and the cycle taking longer to resolve. Inquirers who pull this card will dream a lot more than normal. It is said that answers are often found in dreams, so take heed of these dreams, but never blur the line between illusion and reality.

The Sun

Key words: happiness, fulfilment, love, happy marriage, engagement.

One of the most positive cards in the deck, the sun brings with it an abundance of energy to enable you to achieve your goals. You finally have clarity of vision to understand your true desires. It is a card that is nearly always found in a spread where one is blessed with a happy marriage. It can symbolize an engagement or represent pregnancy or acquiring children.

Judgment

Key words: change, awakening, renewal, a well lived life, better health, a time for cleansing.

It is now time to take stock of your life, discard anything negative and hang onto what you know to be good or need. This is a good time for change, especially career moves. If you have been awaiting a decision of importance, the presence of this card in a spread will signify a positive response.

The World

Key words: Completion, perfection, recognition, honours, the end result, success, fulfilment, triumph, eternal life.

The appearance of this card in a spread normally signifies the completion of a personal cycle or series of events. This card is not obtained by those who sit around waiting for it to come to them. Just as the fool started off on his adventure not knowing what was to come, this is the end, marking a sense of accomplishment and fulfilment, and allowing you to sit back and enjoy the success with satisfaction of a job well done.

The Minor Arcana

Wands: Usually predict energy, growth, enterprise, animation, and glory

Ace of Wands

A creative beginning, a boost of power, a new business opportunity, Health, a new career, Vitality, a birth in the family.

As with all ace cards something new is represented here. The ace of wands is a good card to have if you are considering a new business venture. It indicates an influx of new ideas. It is a torch that will guide you down a path towards wealth and reward quickly and boldly. It will also come up in matters of pregnancy.

Two of Wands

A kind and generous person, Personal inner power, achievement, creative ability, courage.

A card portraying personal power. Work with someone to improve personal gain and turn dreams into reality. Always remember, it is you that should hold the power, don't let it slip no matter how nice the other person may seem. Plan ahead, there is no room here for error or hesitation.

Three of Wands

Success, wisdom, cooperation in business affairs, trade and commerce.

The beginning of personal gain after a period of hardship and disappointment. Success achieved after hard work. You stand now on higher ground and look back at difficulties in the past, knowing that you will not make the same mistakes again. New actions are imperative to strengthen your position.

Four of Wands

Celebration in moderation, constant hard work to reap rewards.

This card brings with it a celebration of good things that have happened and of holidays to come. But beware, if you let things slide, it will not go without notice. Holidays do not last forever. Keep striving to better yourself or you could start to slide backwards.

Five of Wands

Competition, possibility of a lawsuit or quarrel, obstacles, courage.

Unavoidable problems, either within ones self or with outside influence such as business competition. All problems of equal intensity, do not let them overpower you, form a strategy to overcome them. They are sent to test you, and to overcome them you must stay focused and work hard. But beware – do not let them take over your life as they will lead to a break down.

Six of Wands

Recognition for hard work is achieved, victory, a breakthrough, overcome obstacles, success brings satisfaction.

Good news will come your way. Any problems you may have been experiencing have been overcome. You have used tact and diplomacy rather than force, and the outcome is good. You are pleased with yourself, but don't let it get to your head as this could lead to disappointment.

Seven of Wands

Energy, facing your fear, learn to use fear to fight back, victory, courage.

This is a time for advancement, but it will not come without a fight. Throw caution to the wind and take the plunge as victory will be yours in the end. However, you must believe in what you are doing in order to succeed. Do not compromise your virtues for anything, this will result in you becoming lost along the way. It is vital that you remain focused along this journey in order to achieve a positive outcome.

Eight of Wands

Burst of energy, swift and rapid decisions, new ideas, a test of your ability to deal with stressful situations.

This card marks the end of a period of delay and stagnation. Swift action is needed here to progress. Make your decisions wisely and act upon them in haste as there is no time to waste. Take charge of the situation and go with your decision. This is not a time for deliberation or indecision.

Nine of Wands

Stamina, eventual victory, will to do things despite difficulty, tendency to obstinacy.

Expect difficulties to arise when this card appears in a reading, but know that you will have the inner strength to overcome them. Start putting your affairs in order so that you are prepared for a bumpy ride. Every person has the strength inside them to overcome such difficulty, but it will normally take a major upheaval for most people to find it.

Ten of Wands

Workaholic, An oppressive load, lack of free time.

A once enjoyed success has now become a burden. You have to slow down and take time to examine what is important to you, even although you may be the only one who can do what you are doing. It is time to let go of the responsibility that you have bestowed upon yourself and start doing some of the things that you want to be doing.

Page of Wands

Brilliance, passion for life, courage, happiness, sudden appearance of a creative idea, unlimited passion & enthusiasm.

You have the wild spirit of youth, run with it in order to reach your goals. Important news is coming your way. Dreams have a way of becoming reality if you let them. Work hard and you will not be disappointed.

Knight of Wands

An impetuous nature, well liked friend, things happening quickly, a journey or change of residence.

The knight of wands is whirlwind card that enters your life, does what it has to do and then leaves just as suddenly. It could mean that you are going to change something very quickly, or that circumstances will change around you, forcing you to make changes. Whatever happens, be assured that it will happen quickly .

Queen of Wands

A woman, generous, dedicated & fair, charming but elusive, a good friend, but do not become her enemy, someone who is well liked by all around her.

Normally portraying an older woman who is either helping or hindering your personal life. If you are involved in some project, this card can signify its success. You are filled with new ideas and cant wait to act on them.

King of Wands

Self starter, good leader, reliable, gets things done.

Something needs to be done. Not in an artistic way, but rather a doing way. This card will normally signify a strong manly figure that wants to change the world into the way he thinks it should be, or at least, change you to get rid of your problems. His intentions are good, and his outlook is noble. He is on the right track. A person like this may be present in your life in which case take direction from them. If you are this person, you are on the right track, keep going regardless of obstacles.

Cups – usually predict happiness, love, fertility and beauty

Ace of Cups

The beginning of happiness, inner beauty, good health and love.

Where the ace appears in a spread, it normally means the beginning of something good. However, this something will start off good, whether or not it stays this way is up to you. Work hard at it and you will reap the rewards. Slack off and you will notice a decline. The chance has been given to you, it is up to you to make the most of it.

Two of Cups

A new romance, a well balanced friendship, harmony, consideration for others.

Although this card is often associated with the lovers card, there are many differences between the two. It is a much less powerful card than the lovers card, and does not necessarily mean a relationship between two people; it can also be interpreted as a relationship of two sides of one person. In order to love others, one must first learn to love oneself. When this card appears in a reading that the inquirer is not in a relationship, it suggests that the inquirer should examine his/her own self before they can move forward.

Three of Cups

Good fortune in love matters, you are able to do things you never dreamed you could do, a happy outcome.

As the two of cups will signify harmony between two people, the three suggests people working together harmoniously in a group to achieve one goal. It can also signify any occasion where people have a reason to celebrate as a group i.e. Weddings, anniversaries, community gatherings, baby showers etc.

Four of Cups

Looking at life from a different angle and not liking what you see.

This card brings a warning - Be careful of becoming complacent in love matters. You have to work at it to keep it alive or before you know it you will loose it.

Five of Cups

Loss, sorrow, estrangement, self doubt.

This is a card most people try to avoid. It signifies the fears that the four of cups suggest have become reality. Normally associated with loss of a valued friend due to difference of opinion, divorce or a break up in a relationship. In the picture of this card, three cups are spilled, but two remain standing. Be grateful for what you have left. Don't dwell on the past, use what you have left and get on with your life.

Six of Cups

New beginnings, a gift from the past, a step forward in the right direction.

Although it is not good to dwell on the past, it is not a bad thing to think of the good things in the past as these may help you to make your future better. This card is a festive card, washing away the morbid feelings of the five of cups and making you look forward as another cup is added to your tray. You have taken stock of past mistakes and are now able to go forward in your life, opening endless doors of opportunity to you.

Seven of Cups

Difficulties distinguishing between fantasy and reality, in ability to choose direction in life.

Choices are to be made, but among them are a couple that only exist in your mind. The imagination will provide a fantastic-opportunity illusion; make sure you can distinguish between fantasy and reality in your own mind. Keep your feet on the ground, avoid temptation and don't con yourself – the grass is rarely greener on the other side.

Eight of Cups

A change of direction in your life, loss of love, misery, a need to find something better.

This is a time to move on with your life – but in a different direction. In this card you will see a man walking away from his cups towards a swamp-looking area – this is exactly what this card portrays. You will leave the known (a past that has become stagnant) to wander into the unknown on a path to re-discovery. It will not be an easy decision, but the past is exactly that, and cannot be changed, whereas you can make the future anything you want it to be.

Nine of Cups

A bright future, good health and fulfilled wishes.

This card brings with it happiness, good health and joy. Often called the wish card, the presents of the nine of cups will almost assure that a wish that you have will be granted in days to come.

Ten of Cups

Good family life, friendship that lasts, happiness.

A rainbow of cups – it speaks for itself. A life well lived, contentment in ones self with little regard for material matters, and a lasting peace and harmony that can be enjoyed. Use the time you have been given wisely. Don't go looking for trouble and it won't bother you. Be careful not to become too complacent in this happy state.

Page of Cups

Artistic, gentle, kind person.

Believe in yourself and in your dreams. You can live with your head in the clouds while keeping your feet firmly planted on the ground. The page of cups in childlike without being childish. The Page of Cups' presents in a reading can predict pregnancy or the start of a new and exciting relationship.

Knight of Cups

Intelligent, romantic.

This card will often come in the form of another person or a part of yourself that you need to explore. This knight is a willing and spiritual being with a romantic side to him. He will often finish what others have left unfinished. He is a bearer of news, so expect news to come your way soon. He believes that everyone should believe in their dreams and has no time for people who do not.

Queen of Cups

Boundless imagination to a fault, a happy person, loving, artistic, gentle, good natured.

This card represents someone who is comfortable in their own skin. She is helpful to others in times of trouble but will not share her own problems with anyone. She teaches us that by using your imagination you can achieve, but don't let your heart see further than your eyes as her imagination can run away with her due to a lack of common sense.

King of Cups

Confidant man, has dealings with the law, not without kindness, not shy of responsibilities, a man that demand respect.

A man of mystery; respect him but do not try and love him. A power junkie, he is often feared by those around him. Can portray a lawyer or judge or someone in a similar position to these when found in a reading. If you are having problems, this card can signify that it would be better to use diplomacy to try and resolve them before resorting to more unpleasant tactics. This king often has a hidden agenda.

Swords: Usually predict aggression, force, ambition, courage, strife, misfortune

Note: Every sword in the deck is a double edged sword. They can cut with both sides, depending on the bearer. It can be a tool of justice, or an incredibly destructive weapon.

Ace of Swords

A realisation that you can do anything, rebirth or re-invention of oneself, ability to love and hate simultaneously.

You may have to do something that you don't want to do. There is no way of getting around it, so meet it head on. Remember that within challenge there is opportunity. It will not be as bad as you thought. The time to act is now, and you will achieve anything you desire.

Two of Swords

Think with your head and not your heart, indecision, troubled times need to be resolved, direction needs to be taken in order for progress.

You are stuck in a rut. Some action is required in order for you to release yourself from this on going stalemate. You have the answer, but refuse to act upon it. Ignoring your problem will not make it go away. You have to tip the balance of the two swords and make it come right yourself. A time for decisions that will make great change in your life.

Three of Swords

Pain, separation, suffering

The appearance of this card prepares the inquirer for a period of heartbreak or suffering. It may have already started; it may be waiting for you just around the corner. But it is coming and it will have to be faced. Remember, to grow spiritually we all have to go through a certain amount of pain and suffering. Use this as an opportunity to expand and grow your life.

Four of Swords

Rest , retreat, temporary exile, a change of pace, slow down.

This card is about taking time out to rest and recuperate before taking up the next challenge. It can also signify someone who has been taken out of society i.e. incarceration, or someone recovering in a hospital.

Five of Swords

Loss, defeat, cowardliness, cruelty, possibly an empty victory.

You may have won, but what did you do to win? Were you honourable, or did you cheat your way to victory? Did the opponent fight back or refuse to be a part of this petty unfair fight? This card leaves a sour taste in the mouth of the conqueror and the conquered.

Six of Swords

A journey, a new start, a passage away from hurtful memories, harmony will prevail.

Leaving when all is lost is not always running away, it is sometimes the only way to grow. The message contained in this card is to leave, go some place new and leave all your worries and troubles behind you.

Seven of Swords

Violated trust, deception, betrayal, insolence,

playing both sides of the fence, failure.

Beware; you could be the victim of a confidence trickster. Examine your options carefully before making the next move. Do not be blinded by what you want to achieve, rather think sensibly – is it actually possible to achieve this? This way you can make this card work in your favour. Lock away anything you hold dear to yourself.

Eight of Swords

Feelings of restriction, indecision, powerless, No obvious solution, a prisoner in your own mind, illness.

You are locked in a bad situation and feel like you will never be freed from it, but this is nothing new, you know this yourself. The lesson here is to look and find your own way out. Freedom from this terrible bond lies in your hands, but you must want to be free, otherwise you will remain in this state for a very long time. Abandon all negative feelings and you will find your way out of this hole.

Nine of Swords

Inner anguish, loss, haunting fears, emotional pain.

No one likes to see this card in a spread as it signifies something that is beyond our control. Your mind is playing tricks on you. You cannot change what you have done, so therefore you must learn to accept it and move on. The things that you fear are never as bad as they seem. Make a concerted effort to get out of this rut before you let things go too far and become ill.

Ten of Swords

Treachery, back stabbing, rock bottom, plans gone bad, failure, lost resources.

This card shows a bad time in an inquirers life. You have been ripped off by someone you trusted and have lost something you were counting on. It leaves you feeling like there is no tomorrow. There is no escape from it, you have to just grin and bear it. But just as days begin and end, every beginning has to end, and there will always be a new beginning. This is the lowest point of the cycle, from here things get better.

Page of Swords

Detachment, negotiation, an upsetting message.

Normally appears when some form of espionage is present. Have a talk with people that have been upsetting you as soon as possible. This talk is necessary to clear the air, and when you do it you must be able to accept the criticism that you will receive.

Knight of Swords

Strength, bravery, an aggressive and clever person, shows no emotion.

It is now time to stop talking and start doing. Can symbolise a debate or argument quickly resolved. The person portrayed by this card is not devoid of emotion, but simply chooses not to show emotion. He has no fear, and therefore acts on his ideas without consequence. A good card to have in a reading where the inquirer does not know whether to let a situation go or face it head on. Harness the power of this card and you have a winner.

Queen of Swords

A widow, a period of mourning, a decision is reached.

This card nearly always shows a woman in the life of the inquirer. She has suffered great loss, probably at the hands of a man. She is outspoken and has a sharp tongue. She hides behind a cold wit and can often seem unnecessarily vicious and detached.

King of Swords

A leader, teacher, man with many ideas, a wise counsellor.

This king does not inspire people, he tells them what to do. And they do it, because they trust him. His decisions are always right, and always in your best interests. When this person enters your life you will know all about it. Be fair, trust your judgement and don't lower your standards to suit someone else.

Pentacles: Usually predict money, industry, and material gain

Ace of Pentacles

New opportunities, wealth, the beginning of prosperity, good times lie ahead.

Although this card can signify money appearing from somewhere unexpected (a win or inheritance), it does not necessarily mean that you will obtain wealth, it can simply mean that it is within your reach. What you choose to do with this knowledge is up to you. Hard work and diligence will pay off in the long run.

Two of Pentacles

Change, a new challenge or project.

Change is inevitable but should be careful planned. Avoid overspending, especially if you cannot really afford it. Do not take on more than you can do as this will result in nothing being done properly. Find a balance between work and play.

Three of Pentacles

A time to use skills and abilities for financial gain, approval, success through hard work.

This card shows a job that is both rewarding and enjoyable. A group of people are working together towards a common goal. This is a good time to start a project or further develop a project that has been put on hold. The three of pentacles shows early success in a venture.

Four of Pentacles

Love of money & power, selfish, greed, unhelpful to friends in need.

Change can be good, do not fear it. Remember that gain cannot be achieved without a certain amount of risk. Take stock of your options and make decisions wisely. Sometimes referred to as the card of the miser as the person who does not want change will hang on to everything they have and ultimately this will be their destruction.

Five of Pentacles

Emotional drain, loss of self esteem, lack of vision, self pity, possibly material loss.

Often signifying a spiritual loss more than a material one. You may be neglecting your health. Only you can make the difference. Pick yourself up and get on with your life. If this card appears and you have experienced none of its problems, take it as a warning!

Six of Pentacles
Generosity, kindness, helping others or being helped by someone in a position to help.
You are now in a position to clear all debts and repay any favours. Be generous, help others as much as you can, not only in a materialistic way but spiritually as well. If you are not in this position, expect help from one who is, and take as much as they will give. Remember, if you are the one helping someone else; do not give without boundaries as they will become dependent on you.

Seven of Pentacles
Risk, hard work, possible ruin, take time out.
You have a choice, keep what you have or risk it and try to get more. Take your time to examine all options before you make any choice. Do not enter into anything without understanding the full impact

of your decision. This card can bring huge wealth or financial ruin. The ball is in your court. This card tells us that it is sometimes wiser to push the pause button and examine your options before risking anything.

Eight of Pentacles

A change in profession, enjoy what you do, reassurance that what you are doing is the right thing.

Use the knowledge you have to improve your chances of getting further. This card shows a change in career, possibly moving you more towards a hobby or something you have enjoyed doing more. Pay attention to even the smallest detail. Hard work will bring rewards. Sometimes job satisfaction is more important than financial gain. If you are despondent about a change that you have made, this card tells you to work harder at it; your reward is right around the corner.

Nine of Pentacles

Reaping the reward of wise investments, financial gain from winnings, inheritance or settlements, spiritual fulfilment.

Shows material and spiritual wealth gained after a period of hard work. Can also show material wealth gained by inheritance & winnings. With this card comes a certain amount of self discipline, something that you must exercise as not to squander your wealth. Follow through with any promises you have made.

Ten of Pentacles

Stable family life, good fortune, financial gains.

You have your security, but where to go from here? Do not take chances at this stage, do not wallow in it. Instead, prepare the future generation to continue where you will leave off. When this card appears in a reading where the inquirer is in need, it usually means that family will help you if you ask.

Page of Pentacles

A focused scholar, new ideas and opinions, hard work.

This could be a new job or a promotion with more responsibility or a young person who takes responsibility very seriously and will not be distracted until his goal is reached. It could also be a part of you that needs to change in order to become more successful, examine your situation and see what you have to do to change it for the better.

Knight of Pentacles

Accept responsibility, do the best you can, reliable to the point of being dull.

You need to take control of an event and make sure it goes according to plan, if it does not, you will have to answer for it. The knight of pentacles will rush in balled-headed and create upheaval, but he will always get what he set out to do done. One of the problems is that he may step on toes along the way, and this will not be easily forgiven. Can signify travel or the acquiring of real estate.

Queen of Pentacles

A generous and trustworthy mother figure, full of emotion with an appreciation of life's pleasures.

This card will come to you as a person who will be a shoulder to cry on in a time of need. She is caring and loving and will often be generous in a material way, but will not be able to offer you any sound advice. Take what you can from her but don't expect too much.

King of Pentacles

A confident strong and reliable man, usually married with established financial and spiritual means.

Everyone wants to be this card. He is successful, well liked, stable and kind. He will come to you as a friend or someone within yourself that you need to nurture in order to make yourself more like this card. He is a businessman that follows a pattern that never fails. He can be a good friend, but do not cross him as he will show no mercy.

About the Author

Brett Campbell was born in Durban, South Africa in 1967. At the age of 23, he discovered that he had a certain psychic ability and worked as a trans-medium for three years before developing a passion for Tarot cards. Brett currently lives in the Republic of Ireland with his wife Sylvia and their son Dylan.